# The Magic School Bus
# on the Ocean Floor

# The Magic School Bus
# on the Ocean Floor

By Joanna Cole   Illustrated by Bruce Degen

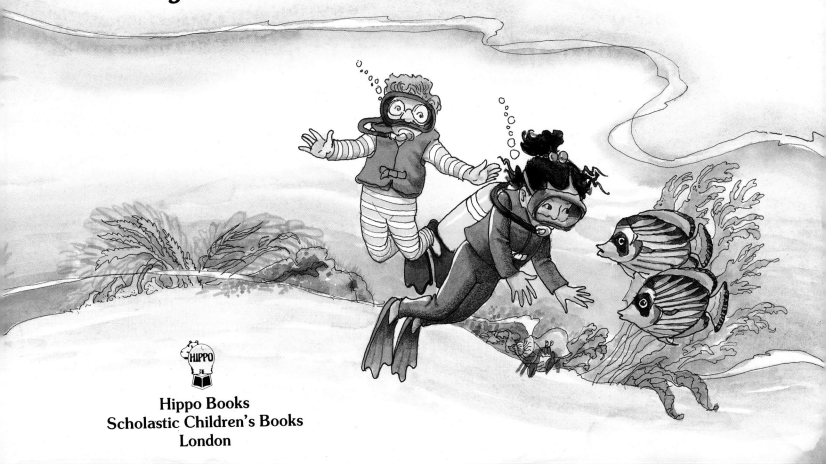

Hippo Books
Scholastic Children's Books
London

Scholastic Children's Books,
Scholastic Publications Ltd,
7-9 Pratt Street, London NW1 0AE, UK

Scholastic Inc.,
730 Broadway, New York, NY 10003, USA

Scholastic Canada Ltd,
123 Newkirk Road, Richmond Hill,
Ontario, Canada L4C 3G5

Ashton Scholastic Pty Ltd,
PO Box 579, Gosford, New South Wales,
Australia

Ashton Scholastic Ltd,
Private Bag 1, Penrose, Auckland,
New Zealand

First published by Scholastic Inc. 1992
First published in the UK by Scholastic Children's Books 1993

Text copyright © 1992 by Joanna Cole
Illustrations copyright © 1992 by Bruce Degen

ISBN 0 590 55245 7

Printed and Bound by Paramount Printing Company Ltd.

10 9 8 7 6 5 4 3 2 1

The sea creatures and plants are only
labelled on their first appearance in the story.

The author and illustrator wish to thank John D. Buck, Ph.D.,
Professor of Marine Sciences, Marine Science Institute,
The University of Connecticut, for his assistance
in preparing this book.

For their helpful advice and consultation, thanks also to
Dr. Susan Snyder, Programme Director, Teacher Preparation
and Enrichment, National Science Foundation; Dr. Michael
Reeve, Division of Ocean Sciences, National Science
Foundation; Cindy Strong, Professor of Marine Biology,
Bowling Green State University; Mr. Maxwell Cohen; and the
staff at the National Aquarium, Baltimore; the Thames
Science Center, New London, Connecticut; and the American
Museum of Natural History.

To Margo, Bruce, Emily, and Beth, with love
J.C.

For Mom and Dad and summer days at the beach
B.D.

It was the end of the day,
and it was *hot* in school.
We had been working for hours
on our ocean science projects.
All our work made Ms Frizzle very happy.
But it made *us* very tired and hot.

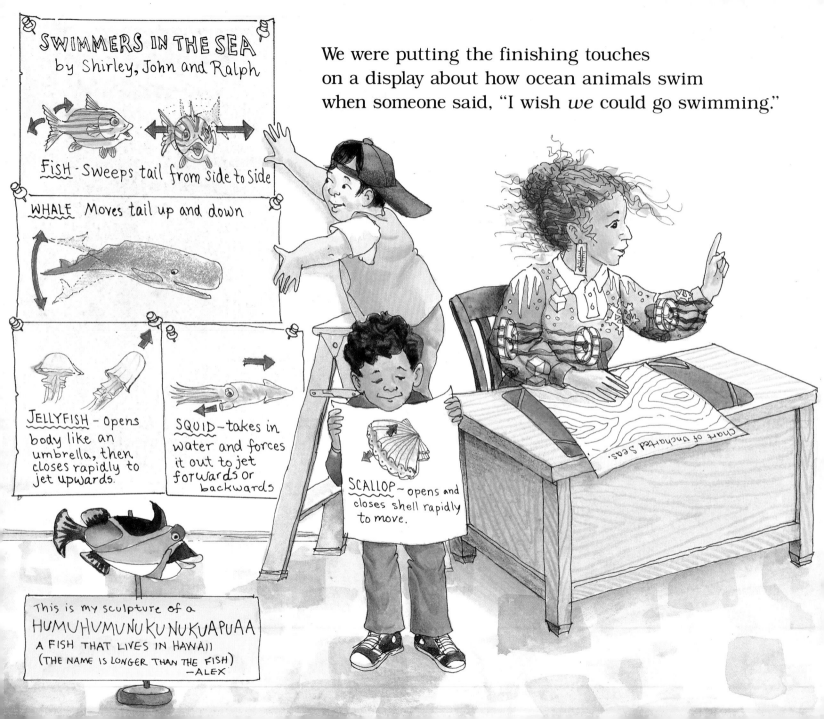

**SWIMMERS IN THE SEA**
by Shirley, John and Ralph

FISH - Sweeps tail from side to side

WHALE Moves tail up and down

JELLYFISH - opens body like an umbrella, then closes rapidly to jet upwards.

SQUID - takes in water and forces it out to jet forwards or backwards

SCALLOP - opens and closes shell rapidly to move.

This is my sculpture of a HUMUHUMUNUKUNUKUAPUAA A FISH THAT LIVES IN HAWAII (THE NAME IS LONGER THAN THE FISH) —ALEX

Chart of uncharted seas.

We were putting the finishing touches on a display about how ocean animals swim when someone said, "I wish *we* could go swimming."

Ms Frizzle looked up.
Without warning, she said,
"As a matter of fact, children,
I've been planning a class trip to the ocean
for tomorrow."
Everybody cheered.
Sometimes having a weird teacher isn't too bad!

DID SHE SAY OCEAN?

WHERE WE CAN SWIM AND PLAY?

DOES SHE MEAN IT?

DON'T ASK, JUST PACK YOUR BEACH BAG!

WHY IS THE OCEAN SALTY?
by Tim
Much of the salt in the ocean water comes from rocks. Rocks have salt in them. When rocks are worn down by water, the salt goes into the water.

SALT 1 LB.
SALT 1 LB.

12"

12"     12"

One cubic foot of seawater has over 2 pounds of salt in it.

MOST OF THE SALT IN THE OCEAN IS THE SAME KIND WE PUT ON FOOD.

SALADS     HOT LUNCH

The next day, everyone turned up
in bathing suits.
We boarded the old school bus,
and Frizzle started the engine.
We were ready for a day of
fun in the sun!

When we finally arrived at the beach,
we wanted to jump off the bus.
But guess what?
Ms Frizzle didn't stop.
She kept going straight on —
past the lifeguard station,
across the sand,
and down to the water's edge.

WHERE DOES SAND COME FROM?
by Phoebe
Sand is formed when rocks break apart and crumble into bits. Each grain of sand is really a tiny piece of rock or shell.

HI! I'M LENNY THE LIFEGUARD. HERE'S A PICTURE OF ME SAVING A THIRD-YEAR LAST SUMMER.

Mm-Hm

HEY, WHERE ARE WE GOING?

ISN'T SHE SUPPOSED TO PARK IN THE CAR PARK?

Mm-Hm

LENNY'S LIFEGUARD SCRAPBOOK

LIFEGUARD

WIND, SAND, AND STARFISH

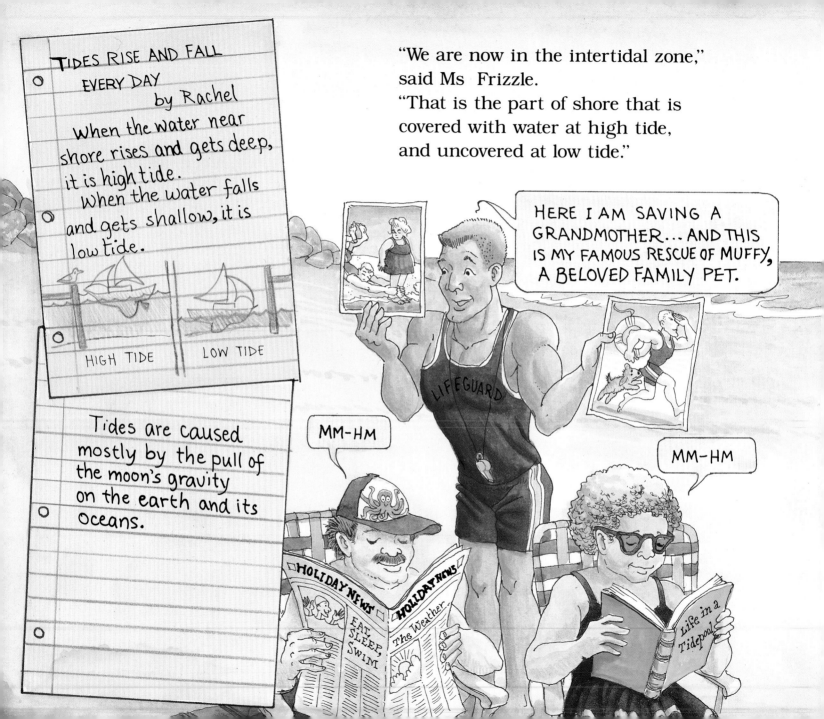

TIDES RISE AND FALL
EVERY DAY
by Rachel

When the water near shore rises and gets deep, it is high tide.
When the water falls and gets shallow, it is low tide.

HIGH TIDE     LOW TIDE

Tides are caused mostly by the pull of the moon's gravity on the earth and its oceans.

"We are now in the intertidal zone," said Ms Frizzle.
"That is the part of shore that is covered with water at high tide, and uncovered at low tide."

HERE I AM SAVING A GRANDMOTHER... AND THIS IS MY FAMOUS RESCUE OF MUFFY, A BELOVED FAMILY PET.

MM-HM

MM-HM

Through the windows we saw tide pools —
puddles of water left on shore
when the tide goes out.
We were hoping the Friz would let us out,
but no such luck.
She kept driving full speed ahead.

SHE _SAID_ WE WERE GOING TO THE BEACH.

NO, SHE DIDN'T. SHE SAID WE WERE
GOING TO THE _OCEAN_.

I SUPPOSE SHE REALLY MEANT IT!

WE ARE HERE
SS SCHOOL BUS
TIDE POOL
HIGH TIDE
LOW TIDE
INTERTIDAL ZONE

Periwinkles

Barnacles

Mussels

Star Fish

Seaweeds

Limpets

Green Crabs

Sea Urchins

Suddenly a mysterious wave rose up.
Ms Frizzle opened the door of the bus,
and the lifeguard was swept inside.
Through the windows
we saw nothing but rushing water.
We screamed and closed our eyes.

HOW CAN FISH BREATHE UNDERWATER?
by Amanda Jane

People have lungs that take oxygen from air. Fish have gills that can take oxygen from water.

OXYGEN DISSOLVED IN WATER

WATER

WATER

GILLS TAKE IN OXYGEN

WATER PASSES THROUGH

Water flows into the fish's mouth, then the gills, and out through slits in the fish's sides.

Ms Frizzle decided this was a good moment for us to get out of the bus.
Thank goodness we had air tanks!
All around us were fish, fish, and more fish.
"Many kinds of fish swim in large groups called *schools*," said Ms Frizzle.

Sponges

LOOK! A SCHOOL OF FISH!

LOOK! A SCHOOL OF CHILDREN!

I WISH WE HAD A BUS.

Down below, on the muddy bottom,
lobsters were catching crabs.
Starfish used their arms
to pry open clamshells.
And jellyfish floated past,
catching small fish
with their stinging tentacles.
The ocean was teeming with life!

Medusa Jellyfish

MOST OF THE SEAFOOD
WE EAT COMES FROM HERE
ON THE CONTINENTAL SHELF,
ARNOLD.

I THOUGHT IT CAME
FROM THE
SUPERMARKET SHELF.

Blue Crab

Lobster

WHELKS

Star Fish

Clam

Blue Scallops

Q: WHEN IS A FISH
NOT A FISH?
A: WHEN IT'S A JELLYFISH!
        by Gregory
A true fish has a
backbone, gills and fins.
Some animals are
called "fish" but they
are not. Actually, they
are <u>invertebrates</u>, animals
without backbones.

Here are some of them:

Jellyfish

Starfish
(also called sea star)

shellfish

SCALLOP   MUSSEL   SNAIL   CRAB

**SHARKS ARE FISH**
by Molly
Most sharks are fast swimmers with razor-sharp teeth. Usually they eat ocean animals like crabs, fish, seals— even other sharks.

**SOME KINDS OF SHARKS**
GREAT WHITE →
← HAMMERHEAD
THRESHER →
NURSE →

**A DIFFERENT KIND OF SKELETON**
by Ralph
Sharks do not have bones like other fish. Their skeleton is made of cartilage. This is the same bendable material that is in your ears and the tip of your nose.

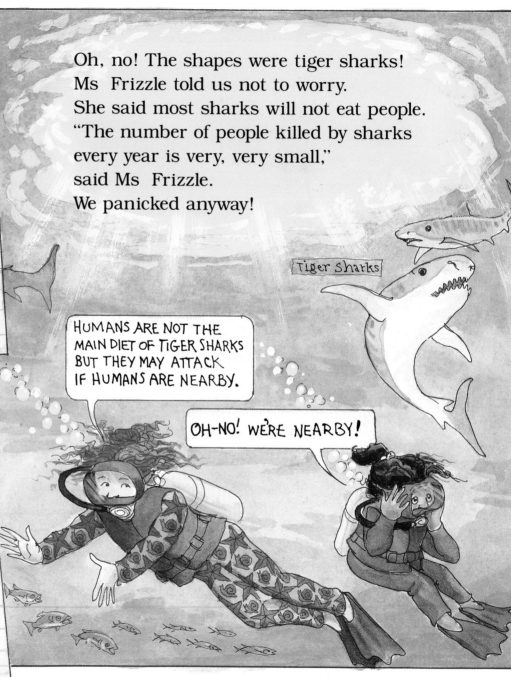

Oh, no! The shapes were tiger sharks!
Ms Frizzle told us not to worry.
She said most sharks will not eat people.
"The number of people killed by sharks every year is very, very small,"
said Ms Frizzle.
We panicked anyway!

Tiger Sharks

HUMANS ARE NOT THE MAIN DIET OF TIGER SHARKS BUT THEY MAY ATTACK IF HUMANS ARE NEARBY.

OH-NO! WE'RE NEARBY!

Then an enormous whale shark slid by.
"Whale sharks never hurt people.
They eat nothing but plankton,"
said Ms Frizzle.
The giant shark swam down, and we went along.
We were leaving the continental shelf, following
a steep cliff called the continental slope.
We were on our way to the deep ocean floor.

WHALE SHARKS ARE NOT WHALES
by Michael
Whale sharks are fish like other sharks. They were named after whales because they are the biggest of all sharks.

HEY SHARK! COME BACK! I'M SUPPOSED TO RESCUE THE KIDS!

WE ARE HERE
CONTINENTAL SLOPE
SS SCHOOL BUS

HERE WE GO!

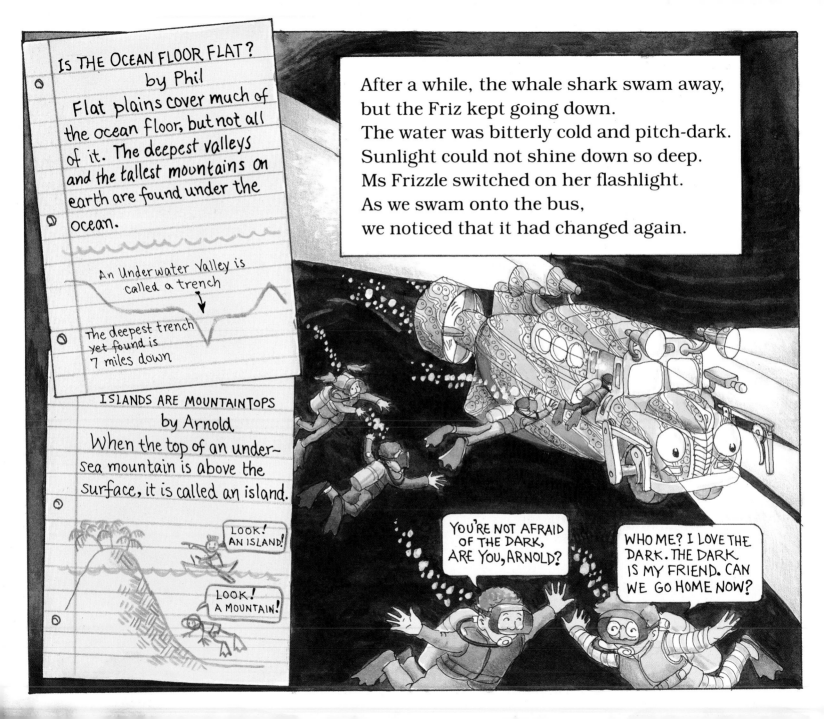

**IS THE OCEAN FLOOR FLAT?**
by Phil
Flat plains cover much of the ocean floor, but not all of it. The deepest valleys and the tallest mountains on earth are found under the ocean.

An Underwater Valley is called a trench

The deepest trench yet found is 7 miles down

**ISLANDS ARE MOUNTAINTOPS**
by Arnold
When the top of an under-sea mountain is above the surface, it is called an island.

After a while, the whale shark swam away, but the Friz kept going down.
The water was bitterly cold and pitch-dark.
Sunlight could not shine down so deep.
Ms Frizzle switched on her flashlight.
As we swam onto the bus,
we noticed that it had changed again.

This time it was a *submersible,* a vehicle made for exploring the deep ocean floor. "The pressure down here would crush an ordinary submarine," Frizzie explained, and she drove all the way to the bottom. "There is not enough food here for large animals," Ms Frizzle told us. "Most deep-sea fish are tiny." The deep ocean floor was as empty as an underwater desert!

WHY PLANTS CANNOT GROW ON THE DEEP OCEAN FLOOR
by Wanda
Plants need light to grow. It is too dark for plant life on the ocean bottom.

WHAT DO OCEAN-FLOOR ANIMALS EAT?
by Shirley
Some deep-sea animals depend on bits of food that sink from the upper ocean. Others use their special lights to attract prey.

THOSE TINY DEEP-SEA FISH CAN GLOW IN THE DARK.

THEY HAVE THEIR OWN SPECIAL LIGHT, JUST AS FIREFLIES DO ON LAND.

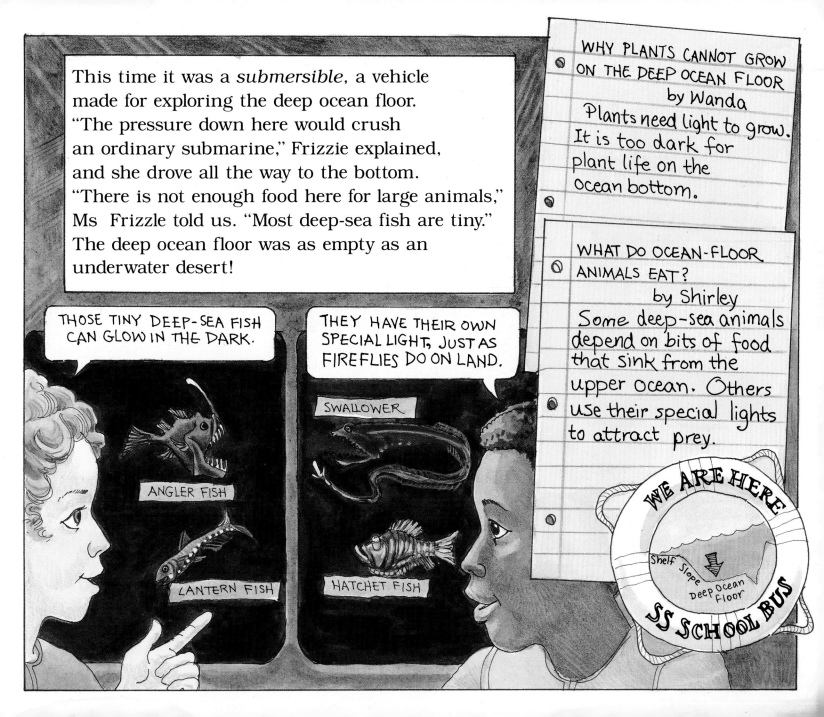

ANGLER FISH

LANTERN FISH

SWALLOWER

HATCHET FISH

WE ARE HERE
SS SCHOOL BUS
Shelf
Slope
Deep Ocean Floor

WHAT CAUSES ?
by Alex
A vent is formed when seawater seeps into cracks in the ocean floor. The water touches super-hot rocks inside the earth. Then the hot water shoots up out of the vent.

WATER

LAVA

HOW FOOD IS MADE AT A VENT
by Shirley
Special bacteria manufacture their own food using heat energy and hydrogen sulfide gas from the vent. This food supports much of the life at the vent.

Then up ahead, we saw a spot that was full of life. It looked like an undersea garden with all kinds of strange animals in it.

"This is a hot-water *vent*, class," said the Friz. "A vent is an opening in the ocean floor. Flowing from the vent is super-hot water mixed with hydrogen sulfide gas."

AT A HOT-WATER VENT THERE IS ENOUGH FOOD FOR MANY LARGE ANIMALS.

THESE TUBE WORMS LOOK LIKE HUGE LIPSTICKS

HUGE CLAMS (1 FOOT OR MORE)

GIANT TUBE WORMS (8 TO 10 FEET)

Ms Frizzle said there were other vents
on the ocean floor.
"Unfortunately, we don't have time
to visit them," she added.
Then she pulled up a lever on the dashboard,
and the bus zoomed toward the surface.

THOSE WORMS LOOK JUST LIKE SPAGHETTI.

DID WE HAVE LUNCH?

PLEASE. I'VE JUST LOST MY APPETITE.

THAT DANDELION ANIMAL IS LIKE A LITTLE FLOWER!

DANDELION ANIMAL (2 INCHES)

BLIND CRABS AND SHRIMP (UP TO 1 FOOT)

MATS OF BACTERIA (30 INCHES THICK)

SPAGHETTI WORMS (UP TO 2-3 feet)

WHEN THE FIRST VENTS WERE FOUND
        by JOHN
The first vents were discovered in the 1970's and 1980's. Before then, ocean scientists had never seen large animals like these on the deep ocean floor.

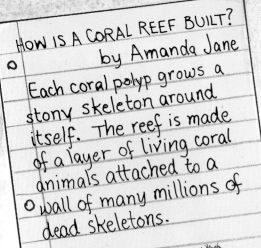

**HOW IS A CORAL REEF BUILT?**
by Amanda Jane

Each coral polyp grows a stony skeleton around itself. The reef is made of a layer of living coral animals attached to a wall of many millions of dead skeletons.

Actual sizes of typical coral polyps

Each "pock mark" is a single coral animal.

**HOW CORAL POLYPS EAT**
by Rachel

Most corals feed at night. Tiny arms come out of a coral's stony skeleton. The arms catch plankton and pass it into the coral's mouth.

ARMS
MOUTH
SKELETON

CORAL POLYP IN THE DAYTIME

THE SAME POLYP AT NIGHT

Soon we were motoring over the open ocean
towards a sun-drenched island.
The bus had changed into a glass-bottomed boat.
Through the glass we saw what looked like
a wall made of colourful rocks.
Ms Frizzle said it was a coral reef
made of tiny animals called coral polyps.
We dived overboard and began to explore.

The reef was made of many different kinds of corals.
Some looked like trees with branches.
Others looked like fans or fingers.
Some even looked like human brains!

THREE KINDS OF CORAL REEFS
by Tim

1. A fringing reef is attached to the shore.

TOP VIEW          SIDE VIEW

REEF

2. A barrier reef has a channel of water between it and the shore.

WATER

3. An atoll is a ring of coral around a sunken volcano.

SUNKEN VOLCANO

WE ARE HERE

ISLAND

FRINGING REEF

MS FRIZZLE AND THE KIDS ARE ON A FRINGING REEF ATTACHED TO THE SHORE OF AN ISLAND.

BUS

"A coral reef makes a good home
for many ocean plants and animals."
said the Friz.
We saw crabs and lobsters,
huge eels and octopuses,
slimy sea slugs and spiny sea urchins,
and the most colourful fish in the world.

SMILE, EVERYONE!

I ALWAYS KNEW I WAS A STAR.

MORAY EEL

GIANT CLAM

SEA HARE

Too soon, Ms Frizzle said it was time to go.
No one wanted to be left behind
so we all climbed aboard.
Frizzle put her foot down
and the bus chugged away from the coral reef.

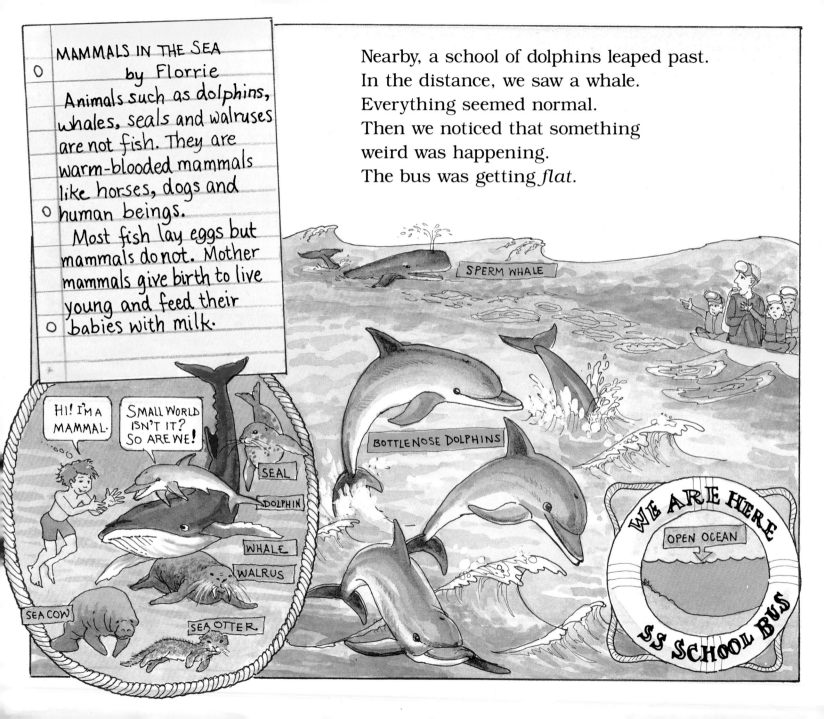

MAMMALS IN THE SEA
by Florrie

Animals such as dolphins, whales, seals and walruses are not fish. They are warm-blooded mammals like horses, dogs and human beings.

Most fish lay eggs but mammals do not. Mother mammals give birth to live young and feed their babies with milk.

HI! I'M A MAMMAL.

SMALL WORLD ISN'T IT? SO ARE WE!

SEAL

DOLPHIN

WHALE

WALRUS

SEA COW

SEA OTTER

Nearby, a school of dolphins leaped past.
In the distance, we saw a whale.
Everything seemed normal.
Then we noticed that something
weird was happening.
The bus was getting *flat.*

SPERM WHALE

BOTTLENOSE DOLPHINS

WE ARE HERE

OPEN OCEAN

SS SCHOOL BUS

As usual, Ms Frizzle was the only one
who stayed calm.
She drove us to an ocean current, and we were
swept along in the fast-moving water
for thousands of miles.
After a while, we saw our beach again.

RIVERS IN THE OCEAN
by Phoebe
Parts of the ocean
flow like rivers. These
moving areas are called
ocean currents.

WHY DO BIG WAVES "BREAK" NEAR SHORE?
by Carmen

In shallow water, the ocean bottom drags on the lower part of the wave and slows it down. The upper part keeps going fast, so it falls over, or breaks.

TOP KEEPS GOING FAST

BOTTOM SLOWS DOWN

"Everyone stay on the bus!"
shouted the Friz.
*On* the bus was right.
It had turned into a giant surfboard!

THIS IS THE GREATEST RESCUE OF MY CAREER.

CONGRATULATIONS, LENNY!

WE KNEW YOU COULD DO IT!

PELICANS

We had to stand on top of it.
And we were riding a wild wave
straight towards shore!

Oh, no! It was a giant wipeout!
The whole class went under.
The next thing we knew,
we were being washed up on the sand.

Our diving suits were gone,
and the bus was its old self again.
There it was, sitting in the car park
as if nothing had happened.
We thanked Lenny for everything
and hit the road.

Back in our classroom,
we made a brilliant chart of the ocean
for the bulletin board.

By then we were definitely ready to go home.
Thank goodness it was Friday!
After that class trip
we really *needed* a weekend off!

FIND OUT WHICH THINGS ARE TRUE, AND WHICH THINGS ARE MADE UP!

# MULTIPLE-CHOICE TEST

First, read the question. Then read the three answers — A, B, and C. Decide which one is correct. To see if you were right, check the answers on the next page.

QUESTIONS:

**1.** In real life, what would happen if a school bus drove into the ocean?
   **A.** The bus would turn into a submarine, then a submersible, then a glass-bottomed boat, and finally, a surfboard.
   **B.** The bus would stay a bus.
   **C.** The bus would turn into a rubber-ducky.

**2.** Is it possible to explore the ocean in a single day?
   **A.** Yes, if you travel by giant clam.
   **B.** No, you couldn't do it in a day. It would take months, no matter how you made the trip.
   **C.** Perhaps. It depends on how long the day is.

**3.** In real life, can ocean animals speak?
   **A.** Yes, but only when they have something important to say.
   **B.** Yes, but too many bubbles come out.
   **C.** No. Ocean animals do not talk.

ANSWERS:

**1.** The correct answer is B. A bus cannot magically change into anything else. It also cannot run under the ocean. Water would seep inside and the bus would sink.

**2.** The correct answer is B. It takes a long time to travel thousands of miles through water. Even whales need months to migrate from one part of the ocean to another.

**3.** The correct answer is C. It is true that many fish make sounds, and whales and dolphins seem to communicate in a special way. But ocean animals do not use human language, and no one has ever heard a starfish tell a joke.

*Joanna Cole* never explored the deep ocean floor in a school bus, but she did spend many summer days at the beach. Growing up near the New Jersey shore, Ms Cole's fondest memories of the ocean include collecting shells and crabs, building sand castles, and riding big ocean waves. Today, Ms Cole enjoys writing science books for children, including *The Magic School Bus* series. She is the winner of the 1991 *Washington Post*/Children's Book Guild Nonfiction Award for the body of her work. A former teacher and children's book editor, Ms Cole now writes full time and makes her home in Connecticut with her husband and daughter.

*Bruce Degen* remembers playing at the Coney Island beach as a youngster. When it was time to get out of the ocean, he always pretended he couldn't hear his mother calling him. In recent years, Mr Degen has visited other beaches and aquariums to see firsthand some of the fish in this book. He befriended an elephant seal on the shores of California, and is the proud owner of two Humuhumunukunukuapuaa T-shirts. The illustrator of more than two dozen books for children, Mr Degen lives in Connecticut with his wife and two sons.